Discover India
State by State

OFF TO NAGALAND

SONIA MEHTA

PUFFIN BOOKS

An imprint of Penguin Random House

PUFFIN BOOKS

USA | Canada | UK | Ireland | Australia | New Zealand | India | South Africa | China | Singapore

Puffin Books is part of the Penguin Random House group of companies whose addresses can be found at global.penguinrandomhouse.com

Published by Penguin Random House India Pvt. Ltd
4th Floor, Capital Tower 1, MG Road,
Gurugram 122 002, Haryana, India

First published in Puffin Books by Penguin Random House India 2018

Picture Credits

10 9 8 7 6 5 4 3 2

The views and opinions expressed in this book are the author's own and the facts are as reported by her, which have been verified to the extent possible, and the publishers are not in any way liable for the same.

The information in this book is based on research from bona fide sites and published books and is true to the best of the author's knowledge at the time of going to print. The author is not responsible for any further changes or developments occurring post the publication of this book. This series is not a comprehensive representation of the states of India but is intended to give children a flavour of the lifestyles and cultures of different states. All illustrations are artistic representations only.

ISBN 9780143440963

Design and layout by Quadrum Solutions Pvt. Ltd
Printed at Repro India Limited

www.penguin.co.in

This is a legitimate digitally printed version of the book and therefore might not have certain extra finishing on the cover.

Hello Kids!

I'm so happy you are reading this book. India is an incredible country and there are lots of things about it that we never get to hear about.

I discovered India because my father was in the Indian army. He was posted to many places all over India—and we dutifully followed him. Can you imagine that by the time I was in the tenth standard, I had changed nine schools? Of course it was hard making new friends almost every year, but the good part was that I got to live in so many places. Right from Kerala, where I was born, to Kashmir, Jhansi, Shillong, Chandigarh, Goa . . . the list is long.

Every time I go to a new place, I feel amazed at how different each state is from the other—and yet, how similar. Did you know that we can see monuments from the Stone Age right here in India? Or that we have more than twenty official languages, and most Indians know three or four on an average? Or even that some of the world's most amazing scientific marvels were invented in India?

Oh, there are many, many, many fun and fantastic things about the states of India, which we simply must get to know.

So get your backpack ready, get set to meet some new friends and join me on a fun trip as we DISCOVER INDIA, STATE BY STATE.

I hope you enjoy reading this book as much as I have enjoyed writing it. I would love to hear from you. So do write to me at sonia.mehta@quadrumltd.com.

Lots of love,

Sonia Aunty

Mishki and Pushka have come to visit Earth from their home planet, Zoomba. They have never seen such an amazing place. Zoomba doesn't have trees and mountains and rivers like Earth does. But the people look exactly the same. When they come to Earth, they meet a sweet old man whom they call Daadu Dolma. Daadu Dolma shows them all the wonderful places in India and tells Mishki and Pushka all about them.

Mishki and Pushka can't believe what they see. They have seen a lot of Earth, but they have never, ever seen a place like India.

They are off to explore India state by state :)

Mishki

Mishki is a curious little girl. She is always asking loads of questions. On her home planet, she is always getting into trouble for poking her nose into things that are not her business.

Pushka

Pushka is Mishki's brother. He loves adventure. He is always ready to try a new challenge. Whether it's climbing a mountain, or diving into a cold, cold sea, he is up for it.

Daadu Dolma

Daadu Dolma is a wise old man who has lived on Earth longer than the mountains and seas. No one knows quite how old he is, but he certainly has been around. He knows everything about everything.

Pushka has been getting his camera ready. He has deleted all the old pictures and cleared up space for new ones.

'I am really, really excited about meeting the Naga people,' he tells Daadu Dolma. 'Are the Nagas very different as a tribe from other tribes in India?'

'Well, the Nagas are very distinctive and Nagaland is all about their incredible culture,' replies Daadu.

'And what about the land itself?' asks Mishki. 'Is the land like the rest of India? Is there a sea? Are there beaches? And what about forests?'

'Slow down!' Daadu says laughing. 'Why don't you wait and see? If you are ready, let's go.'

Mishki and Pushka are ready. They are

OFF TO NAGALAND!!!

A SNEAK PEEK

LAND AHOY!
About the land, water, rivers, mountains and seas.
page 6

LONG, LONG AGO
The story of the state.
page 14

TALK TIME
What language do the people speak?
page 20

A PEEP INTO THEIR LIFE
The music, dance and lifestyle of the people.
page 22

BRICKS AND STONES
Of houses, buildings and bridges.
page 30

STANDING STRONG
Famous monuments in Nagaland.
page 32

WORKING HARD
What work do people do?
page 40

YUM YUM YUM
Food, food, food. What's the yummy food of Nagaland?
page 42

WHAT TO WEAR?
The clothes they wear.
page 46

AUTOGRAPH, PLEASE?
Famous people—past and present.
page 50

ONCE UPON A TIME . . .
Stories from the state.
page 54

Land ahoy!

Wow! What lovely mountains! But there's no sign of the sea, Daadu!

You won't see it either. Nagaland is a tiny state in the north-east of India, nestled in the middle of mountains and hills.

NEIGHBOURHOOD JOY

Sitting right in the middle of a hilly terrain, Nagaland has just four neighbours—Arunachal Pradesh, Manipur, Assam and Myanmar. It's a tiny little state, but it is rather well-known.

FROM THE MOUNTAINTOPS

Most of Nagaland is covered with hills and mountains. The main hills here are the Naga Hills. These hills suddenly rise from the Brahmaputra valley. Then they join another mountain range called the Patkai range. They reach a peak at Mount Saramati.

ON THE MAP

To see exactly where Nagaland is on the map of India, go to http://www.mapsofindia.com/maps/india/india-political-map.htm

BRRRR!!

Nagaland can get cold—especially in the higher reaches. You might even get snow! Closer to the plains, summers are a tad warm. There's plenty of rain during the monsoons. Perfect for its many farmers.

RIVER RUSH

There are some important rivers that cut deep into the land. The Doyang, the Dikhu and the Barak are the main rivers. The Chindwin, an important river in Myanmar, has tributaries that meander through Nagaland too!

FOREST FANTASY

Nagaland has some incredible forests. There are both tropical and evergreen forests—which means there are many kinds of trees found here. Palm, rattan, bamboo and species of timber, like teak, are found in abundance. As you go higher up the mountain slopes, you come across coniferous trees, like pine, as well. Wood and bamboo play an important role in the lives of the Naga people.

The hornbill plays an important role in Nagaland's culture.

ANIMALS APLENTY

Naturally, with a lot of forest cover, there are bound to be a lot of wild animals too. Nagaland boasts of some really amazing wildlife. Tigers, leopards, elephants, sambar deer, many kinds of monkeys and even rhinoceroses roam the lower hills. Smaller animals, like porcupines, foxes, civet cats and mongooses can also be seen.

AGRICULTURE

Almost all Naga families are involved in agriculture. The farmers grow a lot of crops, like rice, corn, pulses, sugarcane, potato and tobacco. But the food the farmers grow is not enough to feed all the people in the state and they have to import food from other states.

JHUM CULTIVATION

The Naga tribes practise the jhum style of cultivation. This means that they clear out land by burning trees. They cultivate it and grow crops on it for a few years, till the land loses its fertility. Then they move to another piece of land. The farmers and their families are not settled in one place for a long period, but keep moving around.

FUN FACTS

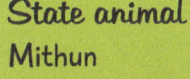
State animal
Mithun

State tree
Alder

State bird
Blyth's tragopan

State flower
Tree rhododendron

WHAT'S ODD?

There's one odd word in each row below. Pushka can't seem to find it. Can you?

| Elephant | Sambar | Monkey | Grizzly bear | Rhinoceros |

| Rice | Sunflower | Corn | Potato | Sugarcane |

| Palm | Rattan | Banyan | Bamboo | Teak |

CITY CITY BANG BANG

Nagaland does not have massive cities. Instead, there are tiny towns—and some are more like large villages. But now, with better connectivity, these towns are growing fast. Let's see some of them.

DIMAPUR

This is Nagaland's largest city. People believe it was the capital of a dynasty called Dimasa Kachari. One meaning of the word is said to be 'big river city' (*Di*-water, *ma*-large, *pur*-city). It has the only airport in Nagaland and its main train station too!

Kohima war cemetery

KOHIMA

This is Nagaland's second largest city and its capital. Kohima was earlier known as Kewhira. It was named after a flower called kehwi. The British built this town to help them administer the Naga Hills.

The Kachari ruins are one of the famous tourist attractions in Dimapur.

MOKOKCHUNG

This is an important cultural and economic centre. It's also the main city where the Ao tribe lives. The government calls this city Land of Pioneers because many accomplished people are from here.

ZUNHEBOTO

Also called Zunhebo in the Sumi dialect, this little town has one of Asia's largest churches—the Sumi Baptist Church.

CHUMUKEDIMA

This town has had many names. Nechu Guard and Samagutin are two. It sits at the base of the Naga Hills. It was an important centre of action during the British rule. There are some lovely touristy landmarks here, like the Tourist Village, and some spectacular waterfalls too!

The Triple Falls which is located close to Chumukedima is a spectacular attraction. Don't forget to visit this waterfall!

TUENSANG

This town is close to Myanmar. Its foundation was laid when India became independent in 1947. Its main purpose was to help the new Indian government to administer the area, which was called **NEFA** (North-East Frontier Agency).

WORD SEARCH

This word search seems to have a mix of cities, trees and wildlife of Nagaland all mixed up. Can you find the following?

- Five wild animals roaming the jungles of the Naga Hills
- Five cities of Nagaland
- Five types of trees found in Nagaland's forests

A	S	D	F	G	J	H	J	K	K	B	L	Z	M	A
C	H	U	M	U	K	E	D	I	M	A	A	S	O	S
E	L	E	P	H	A	N	T	E	W	M	D	F	N	D
Q	W	E	R	H	Y	T	R	R	Q	B	G	G	G	F
A	S	D	L	E	O	P	A	R	D	O	V	B	O	G
Z	X	C	Z	N	M	Z	Z	N	M	O	B	N	O	H
Q	D	I	M	A	P	U	R	B	V	C	X	Z	S	N
X	C	V	B	N	M	M	Q	T	I	G	E	R	E	M
M	O	K	O	K	C	H	U	N	G	I	P	A	L	M
A	S	D	Z	U	N	H	E	B	O	T	O	V	B	T
E	S	K	O	H	I	M	A	Z	X	Z	P	I	N	E
P	O	R	C	U	P	I	N	E	C	V	B	N	N	A
A	Q	F	D	S	A	Z	R	A	T	T	A	N	M	K

SPOT THE DIFFERENCES

Can you help Pushka find ten differences between these two pictures?

13

Long, long ago

My diary is ready. I am going to document Nagaland's history.

Excellent idea, Pushka! Especially because much of Nagaland's history isn't documented at all. Come, let's go back into the past.

HIDDEN IN MYSTERY

There's very, very little written information about Nagaland's history. In fact, most of what we know is made of stories and legends. It is believed that the Naga Hills were occupied by various tribes who coexisted quite happily. The name Naga comes, it is said, from the word *naka*, which in Burmese means 'people with pierced ears'.

The word *naga* in many Indian languages also means snake.

ALL THE WAY FROM CHINA

The tribes living here probably came from China in a mass migration. They soon made their own little tribal kingdoms. These tribes are said to have settled here well before the powerful Ahom dynasty, which ruled Assam and the adjoining regions for a long time.

THE DIMASAS

We get another clue to the Naga ancestry from the Mahabharata. The ogress called Hidimba, who was good and kind, is said to have lived here, and Dimapur, some say, is named after her. The Dimasa Kachari kingdom, a strong kingdom for many years, was believed to have been ruled from Dimapur. There are many ruins from that period that give us these clues.

MOUNTAIN MAZE

Pushka is trying to find his way to the Naga warrior. Can you help him?

ATTACKED AND INVADED

The tribes trying to settle here faced attacks from Burmese tribes, who wanted to take over the lush Naga Hills. Invaders also came to 'head-hunt'—that is to kill and collect as many heads as they could to show their superiority.

THE BRITISH IN INDIA

Around this time, the British decided that they would make India a British colony. They overthrew kingdom after kingdom and soon were ruling the entire country. Before long, they entered the north-eastern hills. They began to spread in Assam and surrounding regions. But the Naga tribes made their life difficult. They attacked many British outposts and frequently raided tea estates and other strongholds of the British.

A BLOODY BATTLE

The British troops were ordered to put an end to the Naga irritation. During the Battle of Kikrüma, many British soldiers lost their lives. The British realized that the Nagas were not to be taken lightly. They decided to ignore them—for some time at least.

CONTINUED INVASIONS

But the Nagas were not be quelled. They continued their raids on British-occupied Assam. Once more, the British took matters in their hands. They set up a strong post at a place called Samaguting, with the specific aim of stopping tribal warfare. Captain Butler was appointed as head of this plan. New headquarters were built in Kohima.

TWIN WARRIORS

Can you find the warriors that look exactly alike?

A

B

C

D

E

F

WORLD WAR II

In 1944, during the World War II, Japan attacked Burma with the intention of weakening the British. But the British troops, made of many Indian soldiers, fought back bravely. A fierce battle ensued that came to be known as the Battle of Kohima, during which the Indian Army lost many men.

FIGHTING THE BRITISH

Meanwhile, there was a tide of unrest spreading across India. The Nagas resisted British rule. They appealed to the British to consider them outside the law so that they could avoid taxes. Too busy with the rest of India, the British agreed. For the next several years, the Naga Hills were excluded from British administration.

INDIA REBELS

The rest of India was still fighting hard for its independence. After many protests and riots, the British were forced to accept that they could not continue ruling the country. India became independent in 1947, and the British left.

AFTER INDEPENDENCE

For many years after independence, the Naga Hills remained a part of what was called the province of Assam. But the Naga people were not quite happy with this arrangement. They felt that they needed to have their own state. They began to protest. The new Indian government agreed to make the Naga Hills a union territory.

A STATE AT LAST

But the Naga revolutionaries were still not satisfied. They were convinced that their culture demanded that they be a separate state, with all the powers that other states of India have. Finally, in 1961, the government gave in and Nagaland became a state at long last.

WELCOME

What an incredible arch!

WEL COME

The Naga people seem to be quite an independent lot. What language do they speak?

They certainly are independent. There are many Naga tribes with their own dialects, but many similarities too.

MANY DIALECTS

Though the tribes speak many dialects and languages, the most common one is Nagamese—a mix of different Naga languages, with a bit of Assamese, Bengali and Hindi thrown in too! Ao and Tenyidie are two other common languages people speak here.

Please come in = Aahibi

Please sit down = Bohibi

Where do you live? = Aapuni kot thaake?

What is your name? = Aapuni laagaa naam ki aase?

My name is Pushka. = Mor laaga naam Pushka aase.

How are you? = Kenekaa aase?

What is the price of this? = Itu kiman dam ase?

Stop = Rukhibi

I don't want = Amaake naalaage

I am going to market = Moi market jai aase

Where has he gone? = Taar kot jaise?

I will come tomorrow = Aami kali aahibo

WORD MATCH

Can you match the English phrases to its Nagamese translations?

How are you?	Rukhibi
Please come in	Kenekaa aase?
What is the price of this?	Aapuni kot thaake?
Where do you live?	Bohibi
Stop	Itu kiman dam ase?
Please sit down	Aahibi

A peep into their life

The tribal culture of Nagaland certainly looks colourful. I think they were quite right to say that their culture is unique.

It certainly is! The Nagas love having a good time, and their festivals, celebrations and dances are really worth seeing.

MUSIC IN THE AIR

The Naga Hills seem to echo with music, song and dance. The people celebrate everything with music. The bravery of warriors, unrequited love, religion, harvest, sowing, weddings . . . everything is narrated with music and songs.

MANY TRIBES, MANY STYLES

There are more than sixteen tribes happily living together in this colourful state. All of them have their own festivals and dances. But one thing is common to them all—the colour and excitement that is a part of every celebration.

TULUNI TIME

This is the most important festival for the Sumi tribe. It's a celebration of gratitude where people give thanks for all they have. The festival gets its name from a drink called *tuluni* that is usually served in a goblet made with banana leaves. During the festival of Tuluni, engaged couples exchange gifts too. There are prayers, songs, dance and food.

TIME TO CELEBRATE

HORNBILL HO!

The Hornbill festival is one of the highlights of Nagaland. It's named after the hornbill, which holds a special place in Naga life. The festival is organized to bring together all the different Naga tribes and celebrate their culture. It takes place in December every year. Every tribe takes part. There is lots of merrymaking and, of course, amazing food.

HORRORS! HUNTING HEADS?

Head-hunting was a ritual in which men would collect the heads of people they killed. A man would prove his bravery to the woman he wished to marry by collecting heads and showing them off to her. During battle, the warrior who collected the most would be praised and be declared a great warrior.

Head-hunting has been banned now! **Thank God!**

SET FOR HARVEST

Amongmong is a colourful pre-harvest festival that is celebrated by the Sangam tribe. The idea is also to bring everyone together. The people pray to their deities, asking for a good harvest. The village priest declares the festival open and then there is much song and dance and feasting!

Nagaland has some of India's most colourful festivals and dancing. The people love to celebrate and no celebration is complete without dance. So let's get set to celebrate.

YO YEMSHE!

The Pochuri tribe celebrates this festival with gusto. It's celebrated after all the hard work of the year is over. The entire village is cleaned by the younger people. The head of each family performs the rituals. There is a purification ritual too, during which homes are purified. This is also the time when young people get engaged. After the feast is over, people get set to begin work on harvesting.

ZELIANG ZOOMER

Both men and women take part in the Zeliang dance. There is a lot of chanting, shouting, thumping and clapping that accompanies this dance. It's a graceful dance that is wonderful to watch.

WAR DANCE

The war dance is one of Nagaland's most energetic and well-known dances. Men perform this dance, uttering fierce war cries, all the while brandishing spears and shields. Dancers need to be skilled, as one wrong step could hurt them. You can just imagine what warfare with these tribes must have been like.

The Naga tribes were proud of their warrior spirit.

TWIN HORNBILLS

Can you find this hornbill's identical twin?

A

B

C

D

SOULFUL SEKRENYI

Sekrenyi, celebrated by the Angami Naga tribe, is meant to purify the body and soul. In a ritual called *kizie*, men bathe in the village well. *Thekra hie* is the ritual when men and women sit together and sing traditional songs. Food and drink is in plenty.

NAZU NOW!

This is a fun festival celebrated by the Pochuri tribe. It's less about prayer and rituals and more about celebrating life. Foot-tapping music, entertaining dance and lots of food is what this festival is full of. And it goes on for ten whole days! Wow! The Nagas sure know how to celebrate.

COOL KUKUYIPHETHO

This dance is known for its amazing steps and music. It's a complex dance with very fast footwork, so the dancers need to be really skilful. They dance to songs that are sung in various octaves, making the entire performance quite a spectacle.

NOKINKETER TSUNGSANG

This is one of the more serious dances. Performed by the Ao tribe, the dance was performed by victorious warriors, who celebrated their victory. Some would wear enemy heads as trophies. The steps of the dance involved much feet thumping, symbolizing that they were crushing the enemy below their feet. Sounds rather violent!

Winning a battle was a big deal and victories were celebrated in a big way.

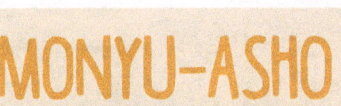

MONYU-ASHO

A tribe called the Phom Nagas celebrate a festival called *Monyu*. The dances performed during this festival are called *Monyu-Asho*. During this festival, tribes celebrate the ancient custom of head-hunting. They wear brass replicas of human heads as headgear, carry weapons and dance fiercely. Oh, scary!

CHANG LO CHANTS

The Chang tribe perform this dance. Also known as *sua lua*, this dance used to be a victory dance after the tribe had won a battle with another tribe. Now, it is performed during a three-day festival called *Poangelam*. Though this is also a harvest festival, the dancers wear warrior costumes and their props are weapons. So you could say this is a mix of war and farming celebrations.

Bricks and stones

I wonder what kind of homes the Naga tribes built. Did they ever settle in one place or were they nomads?

Well, those tribes who practise jhum settle in one place for a few years at a time. But there are others who live in the same place for ever. But in either case, the homes they built were simple and easy to construct.

THE NEED OF THE HOUR

It can get cold, especially in the higher reaches of the Naga Hills. People cleverly built homes that trapped the heat inside. There were few windows and just one door. There would always be a fireplace right in the middle of the house.

A TYPICAL STRUCTURE

Though there are small differences in the way different tribes built their homes, most followed this typical structure.

Akuzu-abo was the 'master bedroom' where the man of the house and his wife slept.

Azhi-bo was the room in which the family stored its rice beer, a drink that everyone has to this day.

Abidelabo was a narrow room in which the unmarried girls slept, safe in the middle of the house.

Akishekhoh was the main room, in which the family pounded rice, and where the pounding platforms were built. In some homes, even the pets stayed here, and so did the unmarried young men in the family.

MODERN TIMES

But all these are homes of the past. Now, more and more, people are building modern homes, especially in cities. Many like to add a touch of tradition too, even though the materials are modern.

Standing strong

Daadu, what kind of monuments can we see in Nagaland?

Well, Mishki, there are not many grand monuments because the people were simple tribals. But we will certainly see some that reflect the history of this state.

KOHIMA WAR CEMETERY

This is a rather elaborate cemetery that is dedicated to the brave soldiers who lost their lives during the terrible battle of Kohima. There are Indian as well as British soldiers buried here. The local people, many of whom must have lost family members, are quite emotional about this place.

NAGA HERITAGE VILLAGE

Special villages have been preserved so we can see how people lived. The Naga Heritage Village is also called the Kisama Heritage Village. It sits prettily in the midst of beautiful hills and you can see the homes and lifestyle of tribal villagers.

The Naga Heritage Village

KOHIMA CATHOLIC CHURCH

There were many missionaries who came to north-east India with the intention of spreading Christianity. They built some beautiful churches. The Catholic Church at Kohima is a lovely structure. It's inspired by local architecture and has a very unusual shape.

TWIN DOORS

In the Heritage Village, you get to see some lovely examples of Naga art. Can you find two doors that are identical?

A

B

C

D

E

DIMAPUR JAIN TEMPLE

This impressive Jain temple was built by the few Jain families that settled in Nagaland many decades ago. It's a lovely structure and tells us how the state has many religions and people happily coexisting.

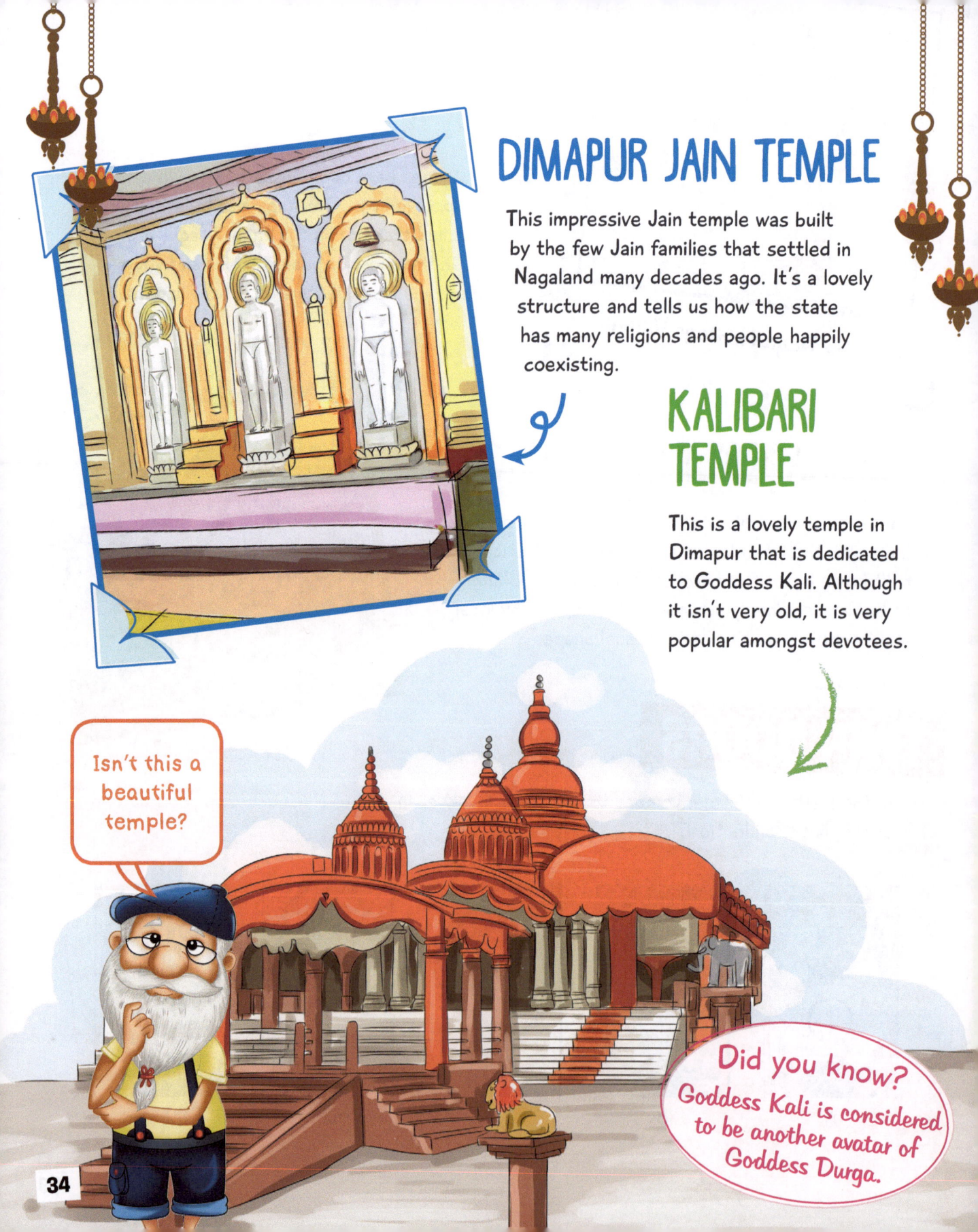

KALIBARI TEMPLE

This is a lovely temple in Dimapur that is dedicated to Goddess Kali. Although it isn't very old, it is very popular amongst devotees.

Isn't this a beautiful temple?

Did you know?
Goddess Kali is considered to be another avatar of Goddess Durga.

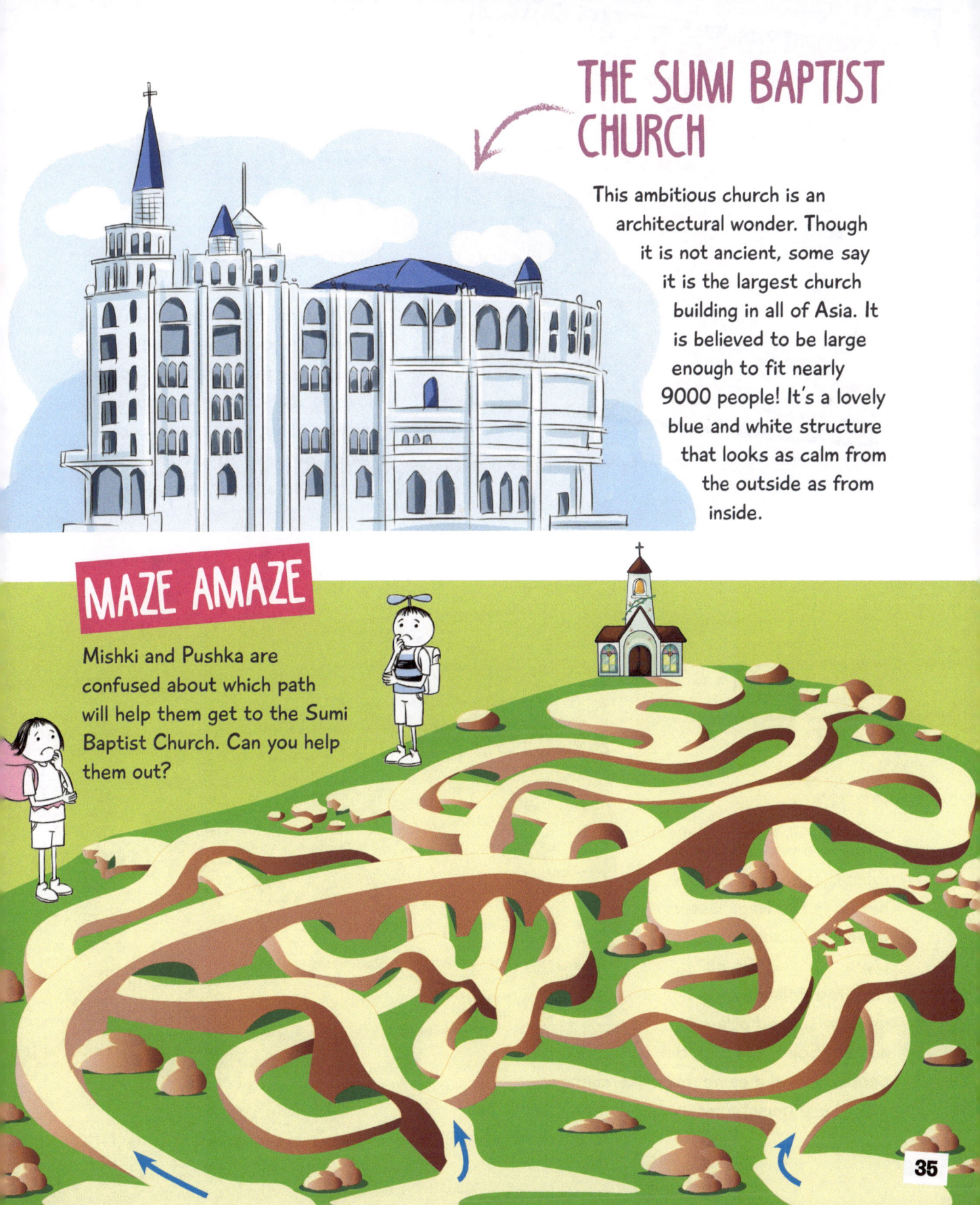

THE SUMI BAPTIST CHURCH

This ambitious church is an architectural wonder. Though it is not ancient, some say it is the largest church building in all of Asia. It is believed to be large enough to fit nearly 9000 people! It's a lovely blue and white structure that looks as calm from the outside as from inside.

MAZE AMAZE

Mishki and Pushka are confused about which path will help them get to the Sumi Baptist Church. Can you help them out?

DIEZEPHE CRAFT VILLAGE

This is a small village that is made entirely for the craftsmen of Nagaland. Only highly skilled weavers, wood carvers and bamboo and cane artists live here. Tourists love to visit this village, not just to see how these skilled people work, but also to buy and take home some lovely mementos.

THE DIMASA KACHARI RUINS

These are very ancient ruins that tell us about a period in the Naga history when the Dimasa Kachari Dynasty ruled. Standing here is a collection of unusual-shaped pillars and domes. Some say that the people played a game much like chess with these mushroom-shaped domes.

Sadly, many of these amazing structures are now in ruins.

TOUPHEMA VILLAGE

This charming village was yet another village created to keep the traditions and architecture of the ancient Naga tribes alive. Built by the local community, it has Naga huts with every detail just like the Naga tribes have in their own homes. And guess what! You can actually stay in these huts if you like. Isn't that amazing?

THE HERITAGE DC BUNGALOW

This is an old bungalow, built during the British occupation of the Naga Hills. The inside of the bungalow is full of tribal artefacts. So for a quick visit into the Naga history, it's a great idea to visit this bungalow if you ever do go to Nagaland.

RHYME TIME

Mishki wants to make up a really nice rhyme about Nagaland. She needs four rhyming words for each word given below. Can you help out?

Craft: _____ _____ _____ _____

War: _____ _____ _____ _____

Weave: _____ _____ _____ _____

Pray: _____ _____ _____ _____

Mishki and Pushka love puzzles. They're excited because they've found a treasure of word puzzles, all to do with Nagaland. How many of these can you solve?

WORD SUDOKU

Time to think. It's springtime in Nagaland. Can you fill in the Sudoku puzzle? Ensure that every row, column and mini-grid have the letters SPRING. Go ahead! Figure out the logic.

		P	I		
I					P
	P			R	
	I			G	
S					G
		R	N		

WHAT'S THE WORD

Pushka is trying to remember all that he's heard about Nagaland so far, but as always, he's all mixed up. Can you help him out?

1. The Kalibari _____ is dedicated to goddess Kali.

2. It's the second largest city in Nagaland _____.

3. The war cemetery in _____ is a really famous place.

4. Diezephe is a lovely_____ Village.

5. The Sumi Baptist Church is one of the largest in _____.

WORD LADDER

Winters in Nagaland can get chilly. Can you help change the word CHILL to PIE. You have to change or drop one letter as you go up the ladder. Look at the clues for help.

PIE

_____ Something that means a dump of things one on top of the other

_____ Something you pop when you aren't feeling well

_____ Something you pay after you've eaten at a restaurant

_____ Something you climb, that the Nagas have a lot of

CHILL

HIDDEN WORDS

Touphema is such a big word. Can you find ten smaller words hidden inside it?

TOUPHEMA

MAT _____ _____ _____ _____

_____ _____ _____ _____ _____

_____ _____ _____

Working hard

I would love to learn a skill like weaving. Because I think I could live forever in one of Nagaland's lovely villages.

Well, that's not all that people do here, although you will see that the Nagas are naturally very good with their hands. Let's see what else people here do for a living.

WOOD WORKS

The large number of forests give employment to people. Cutting timber and bamboo, and converting it for use is a major occupation.

40

HANDY HANDICRAFT

As we've seen, the Nagas are a skilful lot. They weave wonderful fabric that is converted into shawls, jackets and dresses too. There are also bamboo weavers, who make lovely objects with cane and bamboo, such as baskets, hats, belts, mats and a whole lot more.

FARM FRESH

Most of the people of Nagaland are farmers—either growing crops or working in a field. Farmers grow a lot of things, like rice, millet, potato, sugarcane and so on. There are smaller factories in which these crops are processed to make flour, oil, jaggery and other types of foods. So people work in these factories too!

SMALL-SCALE INDUSTRY

People work in small businesses and factories manufacturing paper, furniture, foodstuffs and molasses. There aren't many but are enough to keep people occupied.

Yum yum yum

TREE TOMATO
Solanum betaceum

Khuvie
schoenoprasum

CABBAGE
Brassica capitata

PEA
Pisum sativum

NAGA KING CHILLI
*Capsicum chinense
Frutens*

My tummy is rumbling now, Daadu. I don't think I can visit any more places unless I eat something first.

Well, it is time to explore Nagaland's food anyway, so you can cheer up. But be ready for some adventurous dishes, because that's what you will find here.

COMMON TO ALL

The Naga cuisine uses a lot of unique ingredients that are common to all their dishes. Let's look at some.

BAMBOO SHOOT

You'll find bamboo shoot in many dishes in Nagaland. People add it to meat, to vegetables, to soups and to just about any dish. Sometimes bamboo is dried and used, and sometimes it is fermented. It's a taste that takes some getting used to, but the locals simply adore it.

AKHUNI

Almost every household in Nagaland will have a stock of akhuni or fermented soya bean. It can be dried and powdered, or made into little cakes and stored. These are then cooked along with meat and vegetable dishes and much relished.

FERMENTED DRY FISH

This dried fish is used to make chutneys and other side dishes that add flavour and magic to the main course.

CRACK THE CODE

Can you crack the code that Pushka has made? He is trying to tell Daadu Dolma something.

C = 1	E = 2	G = 3	H = 4	I = 5	L = 6
M = 7	M = 9	N = 8	O = 9	S = 10	T = 11	U = 12

6 2 11   12 10   1 9 9 5   10 9 7 2 11 H 6 8 3

___ ___ ___ ___ ___ ___ ___ ___ ___ ___

SAMATHU

This spicy dish is made of akhuni and meat. Preparation of this dish requires patience and skill as the food is cooked and simmered for quite a while. This gravy-like dish is had with rice.

AWESOME AIKIBEYE

This is a bland dish made of mustard and colocasia leaves. People like to eat this along with the spicier meat dishes that the region is famous for. If you like your food a bit bland, then this one's for you!!

Colocasia is a also a popular vegetable known as Taro root or arbi.

BAMBOO FISH

The Naga people certainly use bamboo creatively. In this dish, the fish is filled inside a bamboo tube and then smoked over fire. It's a different way to cook and eat too!

AKINI CHOKIBO

This is a delicacy, but everyone may not love it. It is made of perilla seeds and snails. These two ingredients are cooked together and people who love it . . . well they love it!

BUSHMEAT BONANZA

The Nagas love this kind of meat that they cook along with various spices. They have it as a curry along with rice.

ZUTHO

Zutho is the famous rice beer that is a staple in Naga homes. Both men and women enjoy this drink and in fact, most people make and store it in their houses. It's had during festivals and sometimes even just for fun.

Zutho is specially served in bamboo glasses.

MATCH IT RIGHT

Match the food to its description. Pushka has figured it out.

Zutho — rice beer

Akini Chokibo — fermented soya bean

Akhuni — a spicy meat dish

Samathu — dish made of snails

What to wear?

I might enjoy being a dress designer. For that, I'll need to know what kind of clothes people wear in Nagaland.

Well, the different tribes have slight differences in their clothes, but by and large all Naga clothes are elaborate. Come, let's see what they wear.

MANY TRIBES, MANY STYLES

In some tribes, like the Angami tribe, women wear a blue and white cloth, draped like a sarong. Some wear a sleeveless top called a *vatchi*, a petticoat called *neikhro*, with a skirt called *pfemhou*. The most common garment is a white cloth with bright red and black bands. Some also wear a wraparound skirt called a *mechala*. The women of the Ao tribe wear bright skirts with yellow, red and black stripes.

STYLED TO PERFECTION

Naga men are not to be left behind when it comes to costumes. Their clothes, sometimes similar to what the women wear, are quite as colourful. In some tribes, men wear a short sarong-like cloth called a *rhiko*. The *moyer tusk* is yet another cloth, usually dark blue, that they drape around themselves. *Alungstu* is a costume that is a symbol of prosperity.

BELLS AND WHISTLES

The ceremonial dresses of both and women are quite splendid. The men carry colourful spears decorated with dyed goat hair, their headgear is made of bamboo woven with flowers and feathers, there are arm bands made of elephant tusks and necklaces of wild boar teeth. All these ornaments are suggestive of the strength and bravery of the men.

SHAWL SPLENDOUR

The various Naga shawls have meanings. The *tsungkotepsu* shawl depicts elephants and tigers, the *aomelep su* shawl is made of dog hair and is always red, and the *rongsu* shawl is only worn by men who have successfully killed a mithun.

Here are two pictures of the tribes from Nagaland. Can you spot ten differences between the two pictures?

Autograph, please?

Are there many famous people in this state? I sure would like to meet some.

Well then let's get going. Many of these accomplished people are very talented and have achieved a lot.

MAYANGNOKCHA AO

This writer from the Ao tribe was the first graduate from his tribe. He became the headmaster of the oldest school in his region. He was also the first to translate the Old Testament into the Naga language. Quite an achievement for a simple tribal boy!

CHEKROVOLU SWURO

This skilful athlete is an archer who has represented India in many international tournaments. She also won many medals for India. She was awarded the Arjuna Award.

TIALILA KIKON

She is one of the best-known poets from north-east India. Her poetry is deep and thought-provoking and readers of her poems feel that they have learnt a lot from her work.

EASTERINE KIRE

This poet and author feels very strongly that more people must be made aware of the life and realities of her people. Though she now lives in Norway, she is passionate about Naga literature and promotes it wherever she can. She is also a terrific jazz musician.

TEMSULA AO

This lovely lady is a poet and story writer. She taught English for many years, and then went on to write many books. She has been awarded the Sahitya Academy Award for her contribution to Literature.

TETSEO SISTERS

These four sisters have carved a name for themselves in the area of folk music. They perform folk music from Nagaland, and in fact have been key in popularizing this music outside Nagaland.

They perform all over the world, and are quite famous.

NISE MERUNO

This Naga youngster is quite the musician. He is a concert artist and has played in concerts around the world.

ATSU SEKHOSE

This talented man has designed dresses for many Bollywood stars. He is committed to making the textiles from the North-east popular. He has even designed for the international fashion brand Zara.

IKALI SUKHALU

Ikali is a very talented fashion designer who has made a big impact in the international fashion world. She has showcased her work in fashion shows in New York too. She tries her best to popularize Nagaland's textiles and culture through her designs.

CAROL HUMTSOE

This pretty model has become a national star. Not only has she taken part in prestigious national fashion shows, she has also appeared on the cover of many international fashion magazines.

Carol started her career at a very young age.

Once upon a time . . .

Sigh! I simply love this state. Such a colourful and exciting life. I'm sure their folklore must be just as exciting.

That it is. If you like, I can tell you a really interesting story that elders of the tribe often tell their children and grandchildren.

THE STORY OF THE KONGLIANG

Many, many, many years ago, at a time when gods and people lived side by side, there was a small tribal family comprising the mother, the father and their two daughters. The parents worked hard in the field, trying to grow crops so that the family could eat.

Now the older sister, Oya, was a rather mean and selfish girl. She was nasty to everyone, and especially to her younger sister, Tenu. Oya would order Tenu about and make her life quite miserable.

One day, as the parents were leaving to go to the field, the mother told the girls, 'Get some rice ready. Hopefully we will bring something back to eat with it.'

Oya waited till her parents had gone.
Then she turned to her sister.

'Tenu, you lazy, good-for-nothing girl!' she shouted. 'Why are you just sitting there? Go, get water for me to cook the rice.'

Poor Tenu. She was quiet and timid. She got up at once and fetched a bucketful of water from the well in the forest.

'Hah! That is not nearly enough,' snapped Oya. 'Go and get more.' And she made poor Tenu go many times to the forest and back until every pot and drum in the house was full of water.

Finally, Tenu was exhausted. She fell to her knees.

'Oh, Oya, I am so tired. Please give me some rice to eat,' she begged.

'Oho! You want rice? Open your hand and I will give you rice,' said Oya. Tenu held her hand out and the nasty Oya scorched her with a hot ladle.

Tenu screamed in pain and ran out of the house. She huddled under a tree weeping miserably.

Just then, the girls' parents returned to the hut where Oya sat alone, waiting for them. They were beaming. The gods were smiling on them and their crop was green and plentiful.

'Look!' said the mother. 'Fresh maize and cucumber and lots of vegetables. Where is Tenu? We can all eat.'

'Oh, that lazy girl! She must be cavorting in the flowers while I did all the work.'

Poor Tenu heard what Oya said.

I will never be happy in this house, she thought to herself. She turned herself into a kongliang, which is a bird, and she flitted up to a treetop and sat there.

When the parents reached the tree, they only saw a bird sitting there. They knew at once that this was their own daughter.

'Oh, Tenu!' they cried. 'Come back to us!'

But Tenu sang a sweet sad song in which she spoke of what her fate was. Then she went from tree to tree singing the sad song: *Kongliang kongliang kongliang kongliang.*

The poor parents were heartbroken that their daughter had left them. They understood Tenu's song, which meant, 'Where should I live? Where should I live?'

From that day on, the tribes believe that when the little bird called kongliang flits from tree to tree singing kongliang kongliang kongliang, it is time to harvest their crop. They narrate this story to their children as a lesson on how elder brothers and sisters must always look after their younger siblings.

TRAVEL DIARY

Have you enjoyed this trip to Nagaland with your friends Mishki and Pushka—and, of course, with Daadu Dolma?

Now you can make your own Nagaland diary. And if you ever visit Nagaland, make sure you take pictures and put them in the photo box.

The first place I would visit in Nagaland:

_____

If I could perform one of the folk dances, I would perform:

_____

The one dish I am definitely going to eat:

_____

The monument I think is the most interesting:

_____

The one famous person from Nagaland I would love to meet:

_____

I think the most interesting historical figure from Nagaland is:

_____

The festival from Nagaland that I think is the most fun:

_____

The five words that I think describe Nagaland the best are:

_____

_____

_____

_____

_____

My Nagaland memories:

ANSWERS

Page 9 WHAT'S ODD?

Grizzly bear, Sunflower, Banyan

Page 12 WORD SEARCH

A	S	D	F	G	J	H	J	K	K	B	L	Z	M	A
C	H	U	M	U	K	E	D	I	M	A	A	S	O	S
E	L	E	P	H	A	N	T	E	W	M	D	F	N	D
Q	W	E	R	H	Y	T	R	R	Q	B	G	G	G	F
A	S	D	L	E	O	P	A	R	D	O	V	B	O	G
Z	X	C	Z	N	M	Z	Z	N	M	O	B	N	O	H
Q	D	I	M	A	P	U	R	B	V	C	X	Z	S	N
X	C	V	B	N	M	M	Q	T	I	G	E	R	E	M
M	O	K	O	K	C	H	U	N	G	I	P	A	L	M
A	S	D	Z	U	N	H	E	B	O	T	O	V	B	T
E	S	K	O	H	I	M	A	Z	X	Z	P	I	N	E
P	O	R	C	U	P	I	N	E	C	V	B	N	N	A
A	Q	F	D	S	A	Z	R	A	T	T	A	N	M	K

Page 13 SPOT THE DIFFERENCES

Page 15 MOUNTAIN MAZE

Page 17 TWIN WARRIORS

B and F are exactly alike.

Page 21 WORD MATCH

How are you?— Kenekaa aase?; Please come in—Aahibi; What is the price of this?— Itu kiman dam ase?; Where do you live?— Aapuni kot thaake?; Stop—Rukhibi; Please sit down—Bohibi

Page 27 TWIN HORNBILLS

Identical twins are B and C.

Page 33 TWIN DOORS

The matching doors are A and D.

Page 35 MAZE AMAZE

Page 37 RHYME TIME

Craft: draft, raft, shaft, daft
War: store, roar, bore, more
Weave: sieve, deceive, leave, peeve
Pray: stay, weigh, hay, nay

Page 38 WORD SUDOKU

G	S	P	I	N	R
I	R	N	G	S	P
N	P	G	S	R	I
R	I	S	P	G	N
S	N	I	R	P	G
P	G	R	N	I	S

Page 38 WHAT'S THE WORD

temple, Dimapur, Kohima, Craft, Asia

Page 39 WORD LADDER

PILE   BILL   PILL   HILL

Page 39 HIDDEN WORDS

Here are some of the words you can form: up, am, top, mop, map, hem, pot, hot, put, mat

Page 43 CRACK THE CODE

LET US COOK SOMETHING

Page 45 MATCH IT RIGHT

Zutho—rice beer; Akini Chokibo—a spicy meat dish; Akhuni—fermented soya bean; Samathu—dish made of snails

Page 48 SPOT THE DIFFERENCES